Declutter Journal

A 52 week plan to simplify your home and your life

Innate Press

Ready to declutter?

Join our mailing list to receive a free printable to track your donations to charity!

innatepress.com/donationlist

Table of Contents:

week 1   date:

What are you overall goals for your home?

_____

_____

_____

_____

_____

_____

_____

_____

_____

Sketch what you would like your favorite room of your home to look like:

What will help you to reach your goals?	How will you overcome challenges that come up in the process?

week 2   date:

How will a decluttered home make you feel?

_____

_____

_____

_____

_____

_____

_____

_____

_____

Draw a
disorganized
space.

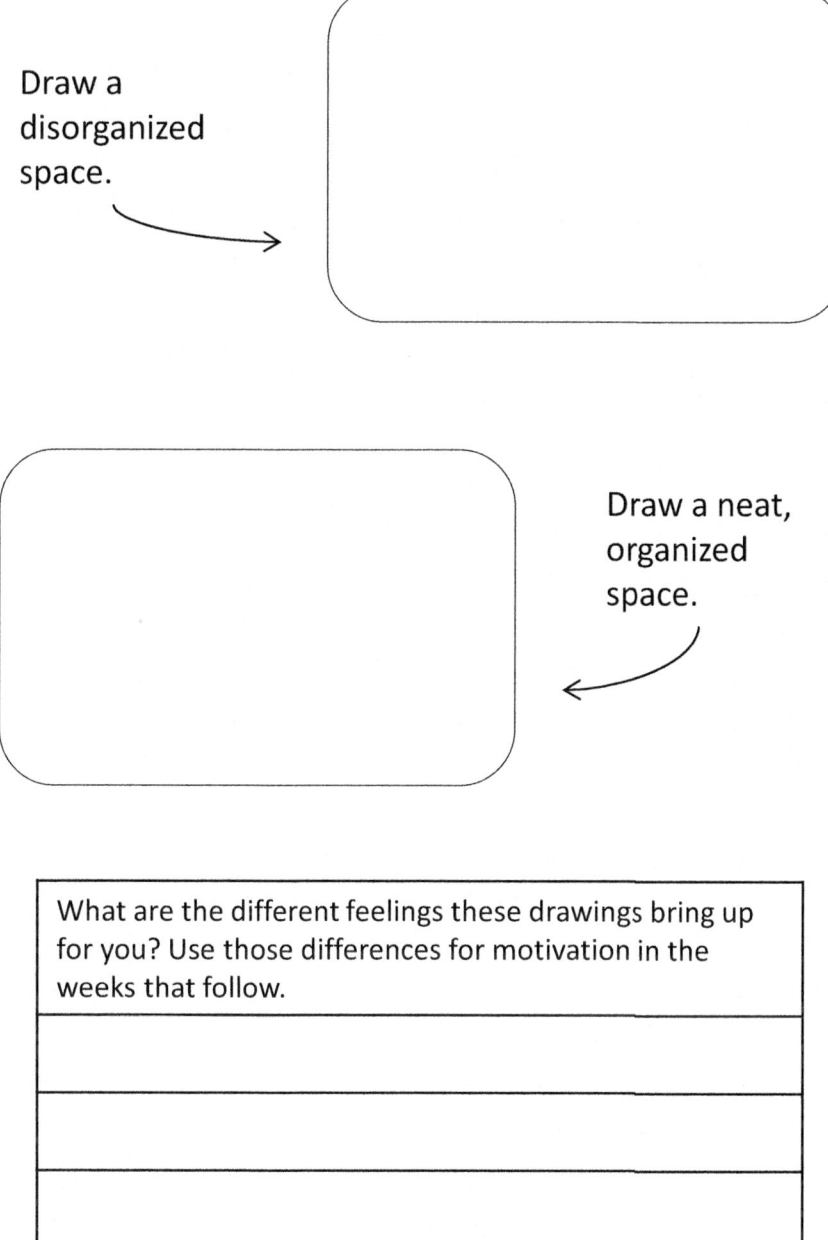

Draw a neat,
organized
space.

What are the different feelings these drawings bring up
for you? Use those differences for motivation in the
weeks that follow.

week 3   date:

Imagine the perfect day. What would that look like for you?

_____

_____

_____

_____

_____

_____

_____

_____

_____

_____

What system do you already have in place that is working for you?

"A place for everything, everything in its place."
- Benjamin Franklin

What part of your day flows easily? How can you replicate that for other parts of your day?

week 4   date:

How can you arrange your home to make your mornings go more smoothly?

_____

_____

_____

_____

_____

_____

_____

_____

_____

_____

What is one thing you can prepare ahead of time that would make your morning easier?

Think about what items you use in the morning.

What do you want out and accessible?	What do you want to be put away and out of the way?

week 5   date:

What would be your ideal way to finish your day?

_____

_____

_____

_____

_____

_____

_____

_____

_____

Sketch what a restful bedroom would look like:

What are the important items to have available as you go to bed?	What are some things you do not want to see as you are going to sleep?

This week's focus: master bedroom (visible)

This week's focus is clearing the visible surfaces in the master bedroom. Let's create a peaceful space! Add your own ideas to the list based on your thoughts during the previous weeks.

☐	Remove clothing from the floor to the hamper or closet.
☐	Place shoes in the closet or on a shoe rack.
☐	Move items that belong in other rooms.
☐	Put donations in a box or bag.
☐	Clear off nightstand of anything you don't use regularly.
☐	Remove items from under the bed.
☐	Keep only a few important items on top of the dresser.
☐	
☐	
☐	

What activities would you like to do in this room? How can the room be set up for these activities?

What do you want more of in this space?	What do you want less of?

This week's focus: dining room (visible)

This week's focus is clearing the visible surfaces in the dining room. Is it easy and enjoyable to eat in here? What can improve things?

☐	Remove objects from the floor.
☐	Consider if you want a rug in this room or not.
☐	Clear off the dining room table.
☐	Put donations in a box or bag.
☐	Clear off the top of any sideboards or other furniture.
☐	Think about reducing art and décor if there is too much.
☐	Keep very few things on the table besides the tablecloth.
☐	
☐	
☐	

What activities would you like to do in this room? How can the room be set up for these activities?

What do you want more of in this space?	What do you want less of?

This week's focus: living room (visible)

This week's focus is clearing the visible surfaces in the living room or entryway. What do you want guests to see as they enter your home?

☐   Remove objects from the floor.
☐   Clear off the coffee table other than a few items.
☐   Keep only a few decorative items on the mantel.
☐   Clear off the sofa other than a throw blanket or pillows.
☐ Arrange any items on shelves in a pleasing way.
☐ Think about reducing art and décor if there is too much.
☐ Store heavy blankets during warm months.
☐
☐
☐

What activities would you like to do in this room? How can the room be set up for these activities?

What do you want more of in this space?	What do you want less of?

week 9   date:

This week's focus is clearing the visible surfaces in the kitchen. Freeing up counter space in the kitchen will make working in this room much more enjoyable!

☐ Consider what is used often and what is used occasionally.
☐ Put away small appliances that aren't often used.
☐ Reduce decorative items that take up counter space.
☐ Remove almost everything stuck to the front of the fridge.
☐ Designate spots for important items (keys, coins, etc.)
☐ Clear off counters as much as possible.
☐ Remove items from top of any islands or carts.
☐
☐
☐

What activities would you like to do in this room? How can the room be set up for these activities?

What do you want more of in this space?	What do you want less of?

This week's focus: family room (visible)

This week's focus is clearing the visible surfaces in the family room. The goal is for this to be a cozy space to spend your time.

☐	Designate one basket for toys (for children or pets).
☐	Clear off the coffee table or ottoman.
☐	Find a basket or bin for keeping remote controls.
☐	Arrange shelves to look visually appealing.
☐	Remove items that belong in other rooms.
☐	Keep the floor clear.
☐	Reduce décor to a few impactful pieces.
☐	
☐	
☐	

What activities would you like to do in this room? How can the room be set up for these activities?

What do you want more of in this space?	What do you want less of?

This week's focus: bathrooms (visible)

This week's focus is clearing the visible surfaces in the bathrooms. The goal is for these rooms to be places where people can feel refreshed and maybe even a bit pampered.

☐ Clear off counters as much as possible.
☐ Remove items from the tops of toilet tanks.
☐ Arrange everyday items in a pleasing way in baskets or bins.
☐ Put away anything not needed on a daily basis.
☐ Consider adding shelves or hooks as needed.
☐ Think about adding a shower organizer.
☐ Clear the floor of stray items.
☐
☐
☐

What activities would you like to do in this room? How can the room be set up for these activities?

What do you want more of in this space?	What do you want less of?

This week's focus: kid bedrooms (visible)

This week's focus is clearing the visible surfaces in the kids' bedrooms. Open space in these rooms makes creativity possible. If you don't have kids, skip this week or spend more time in another room that needs extra attention.

☐	Clear off the floor and remind kids to keep the floor clear.
☐	Keep a few loveys on the bed, but otherwise put away.
☐	Clear off the top of dressers and bookshelves.
☐	Consider adding storage for toys and other items.
☐	Teach kids how to make their beds.
☐	Keep a few baskets or bins for quick clean up of toys.
☐	Show kids the donation box for items they no longer want.
☐	
☐	
☐	

What activities would your child like to do in this room? How can the room be set up for these activities?

What do you want more of in this space?	What do you want less of?

This week's focus: guest bedroom (visible)

This week's focus is clearing the surfaces in the guest bedroom. How would you like your guests to feel in this room? If you don't have a guest room, skip this week or spend more time in another room that needs extra attention.

☐ Clear off the floor.
☐ Take inventory of anything you are storing here.
☐ Decide if you want to use this room for storage or not.
☐ Clear off the dresser or desk other than a few items.
☐ Make the bed with a few extra blankets folded at the foot.
☐ Consider where a guest might place a suitcase or other items.
☐ Add some small items to make your guest welcome.
☐
☐
☐

What activities would you like to do in this room? How can the room be set up for these activities?

What do you want more of in this space?	What do you want less of?

This week's focus: laundry room (visible)

This week's focus is clearing the surfaces in the laundry or utility room. What would make it easier to do laundry in this space?

☐   Clear off tops of the washer and dryer.
☐   Clear off any counters or furniture in the space.
☐   Designate a space to keep items such as detergent.
☐   Consider adding cabinets or shelves in this room.
☐ Keep stray items away from appliances that use gas or get hot.
☐ Think about replacing hampers and baskets with attractive ones.
☐
☐
☐

What activities would you like to do in this room? How can the room be set up for these activities?

What do you want more of in this space?	What do you want less of?

This week's focus: front and back yards

This week's focus is decluttering the front and back yards. Enjoy these open spaces meant for fun.

☐   Pick up any toys strewn about.
☐   Designate a bin for outdoor toy storage.
☐   Remove any trash or old items no longer in use.
☐   Roll up the hose neatly.
☐   Put down groundcover where necessary.
☐   Pull out weeds and trim plants.
☐   Consider what outdoor furniture gets used and what doesn't.
☐
☐
☐

What activities would you like to do outside? What do you need in the front or back yard ?

What do you want more of in this space?	What do you want less of?

This week's focus: cars

This week's focus is decluttering your cars.
When was the last time you cleaned them out?
How about tackling them this week?

☐   Remove all trash (wrappers, etc.)
☐ Gather items that belong in the house and relocate them.
☐ Clean out the glove compartment.
☐ Remove unneeded items from pockets and compartments.
☐ Vacuum and dust surfaces.
☐ Add any needed items (tire gauge, ice scraper, etc.)
☐ Get a car trash can.
☐
☐
☐

What would make long car drives more enjoyable? How about the daily commute?

What do you want more of in this space?	What do you want less of?

This week's focus: master bedroom closet

This is a big one! It is time to go through all the clothes (and other items) in the master closet. You can do it!

☐   Take everything out of the closet (yep, everything!)
☐   Pile up clothing on the bed.
☐   Sell or donate anything 2 or more sizes too big or small.
☐   Sell or donate anything you know you will never wear.
☐ Hang up the keepers.
☐ Organize shoes on a shoe rack or lined up.
☐ Consider all items that are not clothing or shoes.
☐ Relocate these items if possible.
☐
☐

How would it feel to be able to find things in the closet easily? To be able to put things away easily?

| |
| |
| |
| |
| |

Are your visible surfaces in the master bedroom clear? If not, time for a touch up!

What do you want more of in this space?	What do you want less of?

This week's focus: master bedroom storage

This week it is time to take a deep dive into those dressers, nightstands, and other storage items in the master bedroom.

☐   Take everything out of the dresser.
☐   Pile up clothing on the bed.
☐   Sell or donate anything 2 or more sizes too big or small.
☐   Sell or donate anything you know you will never wear.
☐ Fold the items you are keeping and return to drawers.
☐ Clean out other bedroom storage.
☐ Take inventory and sell or donate unneeded items.
☐
☐
☐

Is there a better way to organize the clothing in your dresser?

What do you want more of in this space?	What do you want less of?

This week's focus: dining room storage

This week it is time to dig out everything stored in your dining room and make some decisions.

☐   Take everything out of storage pieces.
☐   Sort by things you use, love, or can pass along.
☐   Look up selling prices online to see if it is worth selling.
☐   List any item that is worth selling.
☐ Donate the other items you no longer want.
☐ Make a mental note of items you don't use.
☐ Next year consider donating what you still haven't used.
☐
☐
☐

Consider passing along serving dishes or other items that you never use. Do you know someone who would use them?

Are your visible surfaces in the dining room clear? If not, time for a touch up!

What do you want more of in this space?	What do you want less of?

This week's focus: living room storage

Look through your living room storage and decide what you really want to keep.

☐   Take everything out of storage pieces.
☐   Sort by things you use, love, or can pass along.
☐   Consider if you have too many of something.
☐   Could some of these items be used in another room?
☐ Donate the other items you no longer want.
☐ If you have books in this room, save them for next week.
☐
☐
☐
☐

Does this room look the way you want it to look? If not, why not?

Are your visible surfaces in the living room clear?
If not, time for a touch up!

What do you want more of in this space?	What do you want less of?

date:

This week's focus: books

If you have few books or have moved to eBooks, you may be able to skip this week. However, many people need a specific focus just on books. You know who you are!

☐   Gather all your books into one space (yes, all!)
☐   Sort by genre (novels, cookbooks, children's, etc.)
☐   Set aside any duplicates for donation.
☐   Visualize how much room you have for your books.
☐   If you need additional space, consider buying shelves.
☐   Only keep what fits in your designated storage space.
☐   Donate the rest to the library or sell at a used book store.
☐
☐
☐

If you are having trouble parting with books, think about which titles are easy to find at the library or contain information that is available online. Let the library store books for you and you can borrow them any time.

What types of books do you read over and over?	What types of books have you moved away from?

date:

This week's focus: kitchen food

Take a look at your pantry or where you store your food. Let's get serious about what will really be used.

☐   Take everything out of the pantry.
☐   Toss anything that has expired or no one likes.
☐   Visualize how you want your pantry to look.
☐   Add bins, baskets, and containers as needed.
☐ Consider labeling the shelves.
☐ Empty the refrigerator and wipe down shelves.
☐ Toss old food, replace the good stuff.
☐ Check through your spices – some have codes that represent expiration dates.
☐
☐

How can you make it easy to grab healthy food from your refrigerator or pantry?

What kinds of foods do you want more of?	What do you want less of?

This week's focus: kitchen cookware

This week it is time to dig through those cabinets and decide what you really use and what you no longer need.

☐   Take everything out of each cabinet.
☐   Consider each item and how often you use it.
☐   Toss items that are cracked or broken.
☐   Donate items that you no longer use.
☐ Think about what you may have too many of (mugs perhaps?).
☐ Reduce items that have only one use.
☐
☐
☐
☐

Do you have sets of cookware or dishes, but only use a few items, consider donating the extras.

What dishes do you use the most often?	What do you hardly ever use?

This week's focus: kitchen stuff

Besides food and dishes, the kitchen often has various other items that need to be sorted through.

☐	Donate or sell unused small appliances.
☐	Toss expired coupons.
☐	Recycle restaurant menus that can be found online.
☐	Empty the junk drawer and sort.
☐	Remove any items that don't belong in the kitchen.
☐	
☐	
☐	
☐	
☐	

Does the kitchen look the way you want it to look? If not, why not?

Are your visible surfaces in the kitchen clear?
If not, time for a touch up!

What do you want more of in this space?	What do you want less of?

This week's focus: family room storage

Hopefully this room still looks clear, but it is time to open up the storage areas and declutter.

☐   Empty out storage spaces such as trunks and drawers.
☐   Donate or sell DVDs and games you no longer want.
☐   Have kid go through the toy basket.
☐   Donate board games you never play.
☐ Make space for activities you enjoy in this room.
☐
☐
☐
☐
☐

Does the family room look the way you want it to look? If not, why not?

Are your visible surfaces in the family room clear? If not, time for a touch up!

What do you want more of in this space?	What do you want less of?

date:

This week's focus: bathroom storage

Storage spots in the bathroom have a way of accumulating lots of stuff. Let's take a look and see what we can declutter.

☐ Empty out the medicine cabinet and drawers.
☐ Toss anything expired or that no one uses.
☐ Replace your toothbrush if it is more than 3 months old.
☐ Store like items together in small boxes or bins.
☐ Designate a spot for extra toilet paper and other needs.
☐ Aim for making it easy to take things out and put them back.
☐
☐
☐
☐

Do the bathrooms look the way you want them to look? If not, why not?

Are your visible surfaces in the bathroom clear? If not, time for a touch up!

What do you want more of in this space?	What do you want less of?

This week's focus: kids' clothes

Time to tackle the kids' closets and dressers. Invite them to help you so you can teach them to declutter!

☐ Remove everything from closets and dressers.
☐ Donate or pass on any clothing that is too small.
☐ Make note of what your child has too much of.
☐ Start a list of what your child needs.
☐ Try different ways of folding clothes to fit in the drawers.
☐ Teach your children to hang up and fold clothes.
☐
☐
☐
☐

How can you make it easier for the kids to put their own clothes away?

What clothing does your child need more of?	What does your child have too much of?

This week's focus: kids' toys

Kids' toys are an ongoing challenge. This might be a category that will never be quite perfect, so be flexible with your children on this. Encourage them to declutter toys themselves.

☐ Remove everything from toy boxes and shelves.
☐ Have the kids decide what to pass along.
☐ Give them a large donation bin to fill.
☐ If possible, pass toys on to younger kids they know.
☐ Encourage them to help kids who don't have many toys.
☐ Let them keep their favorites even if they aren't YOUR favorites.
☐ Consider if you need more toy storage.
☐
☐

What kinds of toys do your kids want to keep? Remember this in the future when shopping for them.

Are your visible surfaces in the kids' rooms clear? If not, time for a touch up!

How do you want your kids to play?	What is in the way of this kind of play?

date:

This week's focus: guest room storage

Although it is tempting, try not to store too much in the guest room. You want your visitors to feel they have room for their things.

☐ Remove everything from dressers and closets.
☐ Determine what you do or do not need.
☐ Sell or donate unused items.
☐ If you have hobby items in here, wait a few weeks to focus on them.
☐ Imagine you are a guest and what you would like.
☐ Consider placing something that smells nice in the drawers.
☐
☐
☐

How can you make your guest room welcoming to visitors?

> Are your visible surfaces in the guest room clear? If not, time for a touch up!

How else is this space used currently?	How would you like this room to be used?

This week's focus: laundry room storage

If you have a laundry or utility room, what do you want to store there?

☐ Remove items from shelves or cabinets.
☐ Think about the likelihood of using each item in the future.
☐ Donate unused items.
☐ Toss old detergents or cleaners.
☐ Look up local hazardous waste disposal.
☐ Dispose of old batteries, lightbulbs, and chemicals responsibly.
☐
☐
☐

How can you make this room easier to use?

Are your visible surfaces in the laundry room clear?
If not, time for a touch up!

What should be stored in here?	What should be stored somewhere else?

This week's focus: pet stuff

Pets bring joy and comfort to our lives, but sometimes also a lot of stuff! Let's boil it down to what is really necessary.

☐　Dispose of old pet medications.
☐　Consider donating duplicate items.
☐　Toss old food or treats that have expired.
☐　Pass along toys your pet is not interested in.
☐ Designate a shelf or basket just for pet items.
☐ Keep a few old towels for your pets.
☐
☐
☐

What are the basics you need for your pets?

What items need to be replaced?	What new items would help you organize pet supplies?

date:

This week's focus: linen closet

This week's focus is the linen closet or any space where you store towels, bed sheets, and blankets.

☐ Remove and pile up all linens.
☐ Sort based on type and size.
☐ Donate your least favorite if you have too many of something.
☐ Consider storing your sheet sets in the matching pillowcase.
☐ Try different ways of folding towels to find the best for your space.
☐ Put nice quilts on display if desired.
☐
☐
☐

Do you have excessive amounts of something? How did you end up with so many?

What items need to be replaced?	What new items do you need in this category?

date:

This week's focus: coat closet

This week's focus is the coat closet or anywhere that you store your coats.

☐ Decide how many coats per person you need.
☐ Remove all coats and pile up together.
☐ Sort by member of your family.
☐ Donate any extra coats that you have.
☐ Donate extra hats, gloves, mittens, or scarves.
☐ Be realistic about what coats you actually wear.
☐
☐
☐

How would it feel to have plenty of room in your coat closet, so you could put things in easily?

What items don't belong in the coat closet?	Where can you move these items to?

week 34

This week's focus: household items

This week's focus is household items such as batteries, lightbulbs, repair supplies, filters, and other items for the home.

☐	Look up your local hazardous waste disposal.
☐	Dispose of dead batteries and lightbulbs.
☐	Dispose of lightbulbs that don't fit your current fixtures.
☐	Toss any dried out materials.
☐	Designate storage areas for the items you are keeping.
☐	Consider rechargeable batteries for less waste.
☐	
☐	
☐	

Where can these items be stored where you can access them easily but keep them out of sight?

Are your visible surfaces in the house clear?
If not, time for a touch up!

What household items do you need to store?	What can you buy as needed?

date:

This week's focus: storage spaces

It is time to tackle the big spaces: basement, attic, and garage. There are four weeks devoted to these spaces. Best of luck to you!

☐	Walk through and take note of the current state.
☐	Create a path through the space if there isn't already.
☐	Rearrange boxes and items until you can reach most things.
☐	Start a list of items that don't belong.
☐ On your list, mark which items should be sold, donated, or tossed.	
☐ Take pictures of any items you are hoping to sell.	
☐	
☐	
☐	

What are the largest items that can be removed for sale, donation, or the dumpster?

What items can you get rid of this week?	How will you get rid of them?

This week's focus: storage spaces

Now that you can access your items in this space, pull out your seasonal or holiday items and decide what you want to declutter.

☐　Gather holiday or seasonal décor and other items.
☐　Decide what storage you may need for these items.
☐　Donate items in good condition that you do not want.
☐　Toss items that are not in good condition.
☐ Protect any fragile items before storing.
☐ Try to store these items off the floor on shelves if possible.
☐
☐
☐

What are the largest items that can be removed for sale, donation, or the dumpster?

What items can you get rid of this week?	How will you get rid of them?

This week's focus: storage spaces

This week it is time to go through camping, sporting equipment, and luggage.

☐   Keep in mind what you used or did not use last time.
☐ Donate equipment that you no longer use.
☐ Pass along sports items that no longer fit.
☐   Be honest with yourself about whether or not you will use these items again in the future.
☐ Donate duplicates and toss things in bad shape.
☐ Try to store these items off the floor on shelves if possible.
☐
☐
☐

What are the largest items that can be removed for sale, donation, or the dumpster?

What items can you get rid of this week?	How will you get rid of them?

This week's focus: storage spaces

This week it is time to go through tools, garden items, cleaning equipment, and other household items such as these.

☐ Gather similar items together.
☐ Donate duplicates and unused items.
☐ Toss dried up materials.
☐ Be honest with yourself about whether or not you will use these items again in the future.
☐ Decide which of these items should be stored elsewhere.
☐ Try to store these items off the floor on shelves if possible.
☐
☐
☐

What are the largest items that can be removed for sale, donation, or the dumpster?

What items can you get rid of this week?	How will you get rid of them?

This week's focus: hobbies

This week it is time to go through hobby and craft supplies. This can be a tough one! Try to be selective and just keep the best items.

☐   Gather similar items together.
☐   Donate duplicates and unused items.
☐   Toss dried up materials.
☐   Be honest with yourself about whether or not you will use these items again in the future.
☐ If you have upgraded to better tools or equipment, donate the older versions.
☐ Try to store these items in an accessible location.
☐
☐
☐

How can you set up a space so it is easy to enjoy your hobbies?

What items are a pleasure to work with?	What items cause you frustration?

date:

This week's focus: gifts and giftwrap

Do you have future gifts stashed away? A bunch of giftwrap saved up for later? Let's take a look at them this week.

☐   Take inventory of the gifts you have saved.
☐   Make a plan for each gift.
☐   Find an accessible place to store gifts and wrap.
☐   Decide what gift wrap and gift bags you will use.
☐ Toss small scraps of wrapping paper or wrinkled pieces.
☐ Try to keep gift bags that can be used for varied occasions.
☐
☐
☐

What upcoming events are there that require gifts? Do you have any that are perfect for those recipients?

Are your visible surfaces in the house clear?
If not, time for a touch up!

What are the pros to keeping gift wrap and gift bags?	What are the cons?

week 41   date:

Whether you have a home office or not, it is time to take a look at bills, paperwork, and office supplies.

☐   Gather papers together.
☐   Sort into piles to: scan, file, recycle, or shred
☐   Scan important papers and bills.
☐   File away papers you need to keep.
☐ Shred anything with personal information or account numbers.
☐ Toss old pens and donate extra office supplies.
☐
☐
☐

Make a plan for handling paper as it comes into your home.

What office supplies do you have too much of?	What supplies do you need?

This week's focus: online bills

Simplifying and automating online bills and accounts can keep your life running more smoothly.

☐ Make a list of all of your online accounts.
☐ Set up as many bills as possible on autopay.
☐ Keep you passwords together in a secure location.
☐ Look at what old accounts need to be closed or rolled over.
☐ Set up auto withdrawal for savings.
☐ Consider going paperless for bills.
☐
☐
☐

Think about how you can streamline your finances using online tools.

What are you main accounts?	When do you usually log on to check them?

date:

This week's focus: email

The ultimate goal would be to keep an empty inbox in your email. Do you think you are up for this?

☐   Go through your inbox and delete any spam.
☐ Unsubscribe from email lists you are not interested in.
☐ File or delete emails that aren't needed.
☐ Send quick replies to emails that need them.
☐ Start a "to do" list for emails that are still in your inbox to remind you of something that needs to be done.
☐ File the final emails and note the date and folder on the "to do" list.
☐
☐
☐

How much time do you spend on email each day? Do you feel this is too long, too short, or just right?

What email lists do you want to stay on?	What email lists would you like to move on from?

This week's focus: social media

Do you use social media? Too much? Or are you wanting to try it out more?

☐   Think about what you value about social media.
☐   Decide what platforms you enjoy the most.
☐   Give up platforms that you don't enjoy.
☐   Consider focusing on friends and groups that give the most enjoyment and value to you.
☐ Decide what time of day you want to use for social media.
☐ Try to avoid checking in during family or work time.
☐
☐
☐

How much time do you spend on social media each day? Do you feel this is too long, too short, or just right?

What social media do you participate in?	How many minutes per day?

This week's focus: computer files

Are your computer folders organized? Have you done a backup lately? Let's take a look.

☐	Clear your computer desktop of old shortcuts.
☐	Put your files in folders in a way that makes sense to you.
☐	Organize photo files by year and month.
☐	Do a backup of your computer.
☐	Schedule future backups on your calendar.
☐	Consider software that automates backups.
☐	
☐	
☐	

How can you keep yourself organized when working on your computer?

What do you use your computer for?	How often do you need to back up those files?

date:

This week's focus: electronics

Do you have a collection of old electronics gathering dust? It might be time to declutter.

☐   Gather old electronics that you no longer use.
☐ Save any photos or videos from SD cards onto your computer.
☐ Consider getting old videos converted to digital.
☐ Clear off any personal information on old electronics.
☐ Donate old electronics that work to charity.
☐ For electronics that don't work, look for e-waste drop-off.
☐
☐
☐

In general, plan what to do with old electronics as you purchase new ones in the future.

Are your visible surfaces in the house clear?
If not, time for a touch up!

What old electronics did you find?	What will you do with them?

week 47

date:

This week's focus: kid art and school papers

This never-ending stream of incoming papers and projects can be hard to handle. Let's declutter and create a system for it.

☐ Clean out your child's backpack.
☐ Take photos of kids with art as they come home with it.
☐ Recycle old lunch menus and outdated papers.
☐ Designate a space for active papers like permission slips.
☐ Scan or photograph old art from the past.
☐ Consider tossing or recycling papers once they are scanned.
☐ Think about making a photo book that shows a child's art through-out the years.
☐
☐

What artwork or schoolwork do you want to keep? What is the reason? How much do you think you should keep?

What types of papers come home from school?	How will you handle them in the future?

This week's focus: large sentimental items

Sentimental items can be tough to part with, but it may be worth it for the space in your home for other things.

☐   Think about what each item means to you.
☐   Designate a box or bin per person for keepsakes.
☐   Take photographs of items and keep the photos.
☐   Consider tossing old trophies and plaques.
☐   Think about where the large item is taking up room.
☐ Consider donating your wedding dress.
☐ Keep antiques and furniture only if you use and enjoy them.
☐
☐

What are your favorite ways to keep the memories of something without keeping the actual item?

What are your largest sentimental items?	What would you like to do with them?

This week's focus: small sentimental items

Small sentimental items are easier to keep, but make sure they are things that bring you positive feelings.

☐ Think about what each item means to you.
☐ Designate a box or bin per person for keepsakes.
☐ Take photographs of items and keep the photos.
☐ Consider tossing things that remind you of a bad part of your life. It may be time to let that go.
☐ Scan important letters and photos and backup the files.
☐ Send copies or photos of items to people who may enjoy them.
☐ Keep special items in a fire-proof envelope or safe.
☐
☐

What makes something sentimental to you?

What are your most treasured sentimental items?	How will you protect or preserve them?

week 50   date:

Now that you are down to what you really love and use, how can you upgrade your storage to fit these items?

☐	Look for acid-free boxes for keepsake papers.
☐	Find baskets or bins that are the right size.
☐	Add shelves where needed in your home.
☐	Purchase good looking storage solutions.
☐	Keep an eye out for ways to use what you have.
☐	Make sure your systems are working for you.
☐	
☐	
☐	

What room is looking the best right now? How can you achieve the same feeling in other rooms?

Are your visible surfaces in the house clear?
If not, time for a touch up!

What did you not do yet this year?	When will you do them?

date:

This week's focus: appreciate and inspire

You made it! You have gone through your entire home. Appreciate all the hard work you have done.

☐	Think about what new systems are running well.
☐	Remember how cluttered some rooms used to look.
☐	Dream about what you can do in your new space.
☐	Share your progress with others.
☐	
☐	
☐	
☐	
☐	

What was your biggest accomplishment this past year?

What rooms have stayed decluttered?	What rooms still need more help?

This week's focus: goals for next year

You have come so far, but decluttering is never truly done. There are always new things coming into our lives.

☐ Plan for future new projects and stages of life.
☐ Think about what you value in your home.
☐ Write a list of what you would like to do.
☐ Keep going and improving.
☐ Look online and in magazines for examples of organized homes.
☐ Enjoy your decluttered home.
☐
☐
☐

What is the biggest thing you want to accomplish in your home next year?

What do you see in your future?	How will you have room for these new things?

Want to keep working on your home?

➢ Go through the declutter journal again to bring your home to a new level of order and tranquility.

➢ Keep your home spick and span with our book "Cleaning Journal: A 52 week plan to clean your entire home."

➢ Keep your house running smoothly with our "Home Maintenance Journal: A 52 week plan to maintain your home all year long."

Printed in Dunstable, United Kingdom